Cool MEALS to start your wheels

Easy Recipes for Kids to Cook

Lisa Wagner

ABDO
Publishing Company

TO ADULT HELPERS

You're invited to assist an up-and-coming chef in a kitchen near you! And it will pay off in many ways. Your children can develop new skills, gain confidence, and make some delicious food while learning to cook. What's more, it's going to be a lot of fun!

These recipes are designed to let children cook independently as much as possible. Encourage them to do whatever they are able to do on their own. Also encourage them to try the variations supplied with each recipe and to experiment with their own ideas. Building creativity into the cooking process encourages children to think like real chefs.

Before getting started, set some ground rules about using the kitchen, cooking tools, and ingredients. Most important, adult supervision is a must whenever a child uses the stove, oven, or sharp tools. (Look for the Hot Stuff! and Super Sharp! symbols.)

So, put on your aprons and stand by. Let your young chefs take the lead. Watch and learn. Taste their creations. Praise their efforts. Enjoy the culinary adventure!

Visit us at www.abdopublishing.com

Published by ABDO Publishing Company, 4940 Viking Drive, Edina, Minnesota 55435. Copyright © 2007 by Abdo Consulting Group, Inc. International copyrights reserved in all countries. No part of this book may be reproduced in any form without written permission from the publisher. The Checkerboard Library™ is a trademark and logo of ABDO Publishing Company.

Printed in the United States.

Design and Production: Mighty Media, Inc.
Art Direction: Anders Hanson
Photo Credits: Anders Hanson, Shutterstock
Series Editor: Pam Price

The following manufacturers/names appearing in this book are trademarks: Pyrex®, Reynolds® Cut-Rite® Waxed Paper, Target® Plastic Wrap, Land O' Lakes® Heavy Whipping Cream, Lunds® and Byerlys® Whole Milk, C&H® Baker's Sugar, C&H® Pure Cane Sugar, Anderson's® Pure Maple Syrup, Morton® Iodized Salt, Wesson® Corn Oil, Kraft® Calumet® Baking Powder

Library of Congress Cataloging-in-Publication Data

Wagner, Lisa, 1958-
  Cool meals to start your wheels : easy recipes for kids to cook / Lisa Wagner.
    p. cm. -- (Cool cooking)
  Includes index.
  ISBN-13: 978-1-59928-724-9
  ISBN-10: 1-59928-724-2
  1. Breakfasts--Juvenile literature. I. Title.

TX733.W34 2007
641.5'622--dc22

                                2006034727

Table of Contents

What Makes Cooking So Cool

Welcome to the world of cooking! The cool thing about cooking is that you are the chef! You get to decide what to cook, how to cook, and what ingredients you want to use.

Everything you need to know to get started is in this book. You will learn the basic cooking terms and tools. All of the recipes in this book require only basic kitchen equipment. All the tools you will need are pictured on pages 8 through 9.

Most of the ingredients used in these recipes are shown on pages 13 through 15. This will help you identify the items for your grocery list. You want to find the freshest ingredients possible when shopping. You may notice some foods marked *organic*. This means that the food was grown using earth-friendly fertilizers and pest control methods.

This book is filled with recipes that get your day off to a great start. Smoothies, scrambled eggs, and parfaits are quick and easy to make. Some dishes can be prepared ahead of time so they're ready to go when the alarm goes off! Other recipes can be made the night before and baked in the morning for a delicious hot breakfast.

Most of the recipes have variations, so you can be creative. A recipe can be different every time you make it. Get inspired and give a recipe your original touch. Being a cook is like being an artist in the kitchen. The most important ingredient is imagination!

GET THE PICTURE!

When a step number in a recipe has a dotted circle around it, look for the picture that goes with it. The circle around the photo will be the same color as the step number.

1 →

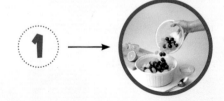

The Basics

Get going in the right direction with a few important basics!

ASK PERMISSION

> Before you cook, get permission to use the kitchen, cooking tools, and ingredients.

> If you'd like to do everything by yourself, say so. As long as you can do it safely, do it.

> When you need help, ask. Always get help when you use the stove or oven.

BE PREPARED

> Being well organized is a chef's secret ingredient for success!

> Read through the entire recipe before you do anything else.

> Gather all your cooking tools and ingredients.

> Get the ingredients ready. The list of ingredients tells how to prepare each item.

> Put each prepared ingredient into a separate bowl.

> Read the recipe instructions carefully. Do the steps in the order they are listed.

BE SMART, BE SAFE

> If you use the stove or oven, you need an adult in the kitchen with you.

> Never use the stove or oven if you are home alone!

> Always get an adult to help with the hot jobs, such as draining boiling water.

> Have an adult nearby when you are using a sharp tool such as a knife, peeler, or grater. Always use sharp tools with care.

> Always turn pot handles toward the back of the stove. This helps prevent you from accidentally knocking over pots.

> Prevent accidents by working slowly and carefully. Take your time.

> If you get hurt, let an adult know right away!

BE NEAT AND CLEAN

> Start with clean hands, clean tools, and a clean work surface.

> Tie back long hair so it stays out of the way and out of the food.

> Wear comfortable clothing and roll up your sleeves.

> Aprons and chef hats are optional!

No Germs Allowed!

After you handle raw eggs or raw meat, wash your hands with soap and water. Wash tools and work surfaces with soap and water too. Raw eggs and raw meat have bacteria that can't survive being cooked. But the bacteria can survive at room or body temperature. These bacteria can make you very sick if you consume them. So, keep everything clean!

KEY SYMBOLS

In this book, you will see some symbols beside the recipes. Here is what they mean.

HOT STUFF!

The recipe requires the use of a stove or oven. You need adult assistance and supervision.

SUPER SHARP!

A sharp tool such as a peeler, knife, or grater is needed. Get an adult to stand by.

EVEN COOLER!

This symbol means adventure! It could be a tip for making the recipe spicier. Sometimes it's a wild variation using an unusual ingredient. Give it a try! Get inspired and invent your own super-cool ideas.

MEASURING

Most ingredients are measured by the cup, tablespoon, or teaspoon.

Measuring cups and spoons come in a variety of sizes. An amount is printed or etched on each one to show how much it holds. To measure ½ cup, use the measuring cup marked ½ cup and fill it to the top.

Ingredients such as meat and cheese are measured by weight in ounces or pounds. You purchase them by weight too.

To measure flour, spoon flour into a measuring cup. Fill the measuring cup to overflowing. Then use a table knife to scrape the excess flour back into the bag or canister.

TIP: Set a measuring cup inside a large bowl to catch spills. Hold a measuring spoon over a small bowl or cup to catch spills.

The Tool Box

A box on the bottom of the first page of each recipe lists the tools you need.
When you come across a tool you don't know, turn back to these pages.

SERRATED KNIFE

SMALL SHARP KNIFE

CUTTING BOARD

MIXING BOWLS

MEASURING CUPS

MEASURING SPOONS

GLASS MEASURING CUP

PREP BOWLS

WOODEN SPOON

SPOON

TABLE KNIFE

FORK

RUBBER SPATULA

SPATULA

WHISK

PASTRY BLENDER

ZESTER

PASTRY BRUSH

SAUCEPAN

SKILLET

GRATER

WIRE RACK

JUICER

BAKING SHEET

POT HOLDER

TOWELS

9 × 13 PAN

PLASTIC WRAP

WAXED PAPER

TIMER

BLENDER

Cool Cooking Terms

You need to learn the basic cooking terms and the actions that go with them. Whenever you need to remind yourself, just turn back to these pages.

Most ingredients need preparation before they are cooked or assembled. Look at the list of ingredients beside the recipe. After some items, you'll see words such as *chopped*, *sliced*, or *diced*. These words tell you how to prepare the ingredients.

FIRST THINGS FIRST

Always wash fruit and vegetables well. Rinse them under cold water. Pat them dry with a towel. Then they won't slip when you cut them.

PEEL

Peel means to remove the skin. To peel onion or garlic, remove the papery shell. Trim each end with a sharp knife. Then peel off the outer layer with your fingers. Never put garlic or onion peels in a food disposer!

CHOP

Chop means to cut things into small pieces. The more you chop, the smaller the pieces. If a recipe says finely chopped, it means you need very small pieces.

SLICE

Slice means to cut food into pieces of the same thickness.

CUBE OR DICE

Cube and *dice* mean to cut cube or dice shapes. Usually *dice* refers to smaller pieces, and *cube* refers to larger pieces. Often a recipe will give you a dimension, such as ¼-inch dice.

TIP: A **serrated** knife is the best choice for cutting bread.

TIP: Use two steps to dice or cube. First make all your cuts going one direction. Then turn the cutting board and make the crosscuts.

GRATE

Grate means to shred something into small pieces using a grater. A grater has surfaces covered in holes with raised, sharp edges. You rub the food against a surface using firm pressure.

WHISK

Whisk means to beat quickly by hand. The tool you use to whisk is also called a whisk. Move the whisk using a circular motion. If you don't have a whisk, you can use a fork instead.

MIX

When you mix, you stir ingredients together, usually with a large spoon. *Blend* is another word for *mix*.

GREASE

Grease means to coat a surface of a pan with oil or butter to keep food from sticking to it. Use a wad of waxed paper or paper towel to spread a light layer of grease evenly over the pan.

ZEST

Zest means to make fine shavings of the outer layer of a citrus fruit. The shavings are also called zest. You zest citrus fruit by rubbing it over the

smallest holes on a grater or over a tool called a zester. Grate only the colored layer of the skin. This layer contains flavorful oils. The white layer beneath the colored layer, called the pith, is bitter and should not be grated.

CUT IN

Cut in almost always refers to working butter into dry ingredients. You can use a **pastry** blender or two table knives to do this. Cut the butter into small pieces to work it into the flour mixture.

After you cut in the butter, the mixture will look like small, even crumbs.

BREAKING AN EGG

Tap the widest part of the egg firmly against the side of a bowl. If it does not crack, do it again. The crack needs to go through the shell and inner membrane.

KNEAD

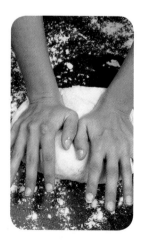

Knead means to use your hands to make dough smooth. Fold the dough in half and press down on it. Turn the dough sideways, fold it in half again, and press down on it again. Continue to turn, fold, and press the dough until it is smooth.

Hold the cracked egg over a bowl. Use both hands to pull the two sides of the shell apart. Let the egg white and **yolk** fall into the bowl. Discard the shell. If any pieces of shell fall into the bowl, remove them before breaking the next egg.

The Coolest Ingredients

ONION

BROCCOLI

MUSHROOMS

GREEN GRAPES

RED GRAPES

BLUEBERRIES

CANTALOUPE

HONEYDEW MELON

PINEAPPLE

STRAWBERRIES

ORANGES

ORANGE JUICE

ROLLED OATS

WHEAT GERM

FROZEN RASPBERRIES

FLAKED COCONUT

13

Allergy Alert

Some people have a reaction when they eat certain kinds of food. If you have any allergies, you know what it's all about. An allergic reaction can require emergency medical help. Nut allergies are serious and can be especially dangerous. Before you serve anything made with nuts, ask if anyone has a nut allergy. People with nut allergies will not be able to eat what you have prepared. Don't be offended. It might save a life!

SUNFLOWER SEEDS

CASHEWS

SESAME SEEDS

RAISINS

DRIED CRANBERRIES

HAM

RASPBERRY YOGURT

CHEDDAR CHEESE

EGGS

BUTTER

HEAVY CREAM

MILK

BAGUETTE

SOURDOUGH BREAD

ALL-PURPOSE FLOUR

SUPERFINE SUGAR

CONFECTIONERS' SUGAR

BROWN SUGAR

MAPLE SYRUP

HONEY

SUGAR

COOKING OIL

CINNAMON

BAKING POWDER

SALT

BLACK PEPPER

15

Razzleberry Smoothies

Put some razzle and
dazzle in your day!

MAKES 2 SMOOTHIES

INGREDIENTS

1 cup frozen raspberries
1 cup raspberry yogurt
1 cup orange juice
1 teaspoon superfine sugar

TOOLS: Measuring cups   Blender
Measuring spoon

1 Let the frozen raspberries thaw for 20 minutes.

2 Put all of the ingredients in a blender. Blend on high speed until the ingredients are smooth, about 1 minute.

3 Pour the smoothie into two large glasses and serve.

Even Cooler!

To use fresh fruit, you need to make a few adjustments. Use 1½ cups of fresh fruit, 1 cup of yogurt, ½ cup of juice, 1 teaspoon of superfine sugar, and a few ice cubes. Blend until the ice is crushed and the mixture is smooth.

Invent your own smoothies! Bananas, blueberries, papaya, mango, pineapple, and blackberries all make great smoothies. Use either plain yogurt or a flavored yogurt that **complements** the fruit. Good juice choices are orange, apple, white grape, mixed berry, pineapple, **guava**, mango, and lemonade.

Variations

> Add 2 teaspoons of fresh-squeezed lime juice to your Razzleberry Smoothie. Garnish it with a lime wedge.

> To make a strawberry smoothie, use frozen strawberries, strawberry yogurt, apple juice, and superfine sugar.

> Substitute 1 tablespoon of honey or 2 teaspoons of confectioners' sugar for the superfine sugar.

> Use plain yogurt instead of flavored yogurt and increase the sweetener to suit your taste.

Rainbow Fruit Salad

Colorful, delicious, and goes with everything!

MAKES 6 SERVINGS

INGREDIENTS

1 cup green grapes

1 cup red grapes

1 cup sliced strawberries

1 cup cantaloupe, cut in 1-inch cubes

1 cup honeydew melon, cut in 1-inch cubes

1 cup pineapple, cut in 1-inch cubes

1 cup blueberries

Juice from 1 orange

2 teaspoons superfine sugar

TOOLS: Cutting board · Small sharp knife · Measuring cups · Measuring spoons · Prep bowls · Large mixing bowl · Juicer · Spoon

1. Put all the fruit in a bowl.

2. Squeeze the juice from an orange using a juicer. Pick any seeds from the juice, then pour the juice over the fruit.

3. Sprinkle the sugar over the fruit and mix well.

4. Chill the salad for 1 hour or longer before serving it.

Variations

> Use any fruit you like! Just cut it into bite-size pieces and add it to the mix. Raspberries and blackberries do not need to be cut. When using cherries, remove the pits. If you use bananas or apples, brush the cut surfaces with lemon juice so they won't turn brown.

> Use fresh lemon or lime juice instead of orange juice. Since these fruits are more tart than oranges, increase the sugar to suit your taste.

> Mix 1 cup of vanilla yogurt into the salad. Or, use any fruit-flavored yogurt you like.

Even Cooler!

Sprinkle the salad with 1 cup of flaked coconut before serving it.

Perfect Scrambled Eggs

Fuel up with a protein-packed classic!

MAKES 4 SERVINGS

TOOLS: Measuring cups
Measuring spoons
Mixing bowl
Whisk
Skillet
Wooden spoon

1. Break the eggs into a mixing bowl.

2. Add the milk, salt, and pepper and whisk until blended. For fluffier eggs, whisk for 1 more minute.

3. Melt the butter in a skillet over medium heat. When the butter is foamy, pour the egg mixture into the skillet.

4. Use a wooden spoon or a rubber spatula to gently stir the eggs as they cook. When the eggs are cooked through, serve them immediately.

Variations

> Top the eggs with sliced scallions, chopped fresh parsley, or shredded cheese.

> Stir 4 ounces of cubed cream cheese into the eggs while they are cooking.

Overnight French Toast

Rests while you sleep and bakes in minutes!

SERVES 8

TOOLS:
Cutting board
Serrated knife
Measuring cups
Measuring spoons

Prep bowls
Mixing bowls
Whisk
9 × 13 pan

Baking sheet
Plastic wrap
Spatula
Pot holder

1. Use a **serrated** knife to cut the baguette into ¾-inch slices. Set the bread slices on a baking sheet to dry out for 1 to 2 hours.

2. Put the bread slices in a 9 × 13 pan. Fit in as many pieces as you can.

3. Whisk the eggs, milk, and salt together. Pour the mixture evenly over the bread. After 10 minutes, turn each piece of bread over. Cover the pan with plastic wrap and refrigerate it overnight.

4. In the morning, remove the pan from the refrigerator and preheat the oven to 450 degrees. Grease a baking sheet with 1 to 2 tablespoons of soft butter.

5. Put the bread slices wet side up on the baking sheet.

6. Mix the sugar and cinnamon and sprinkle the mixture over the bread slices.

7. Bake the French toast uncovered for 15 to 20 minutes.

8. Use a spatula to remove the bread from the baking sheet. Place the slices bottom side up on serving plates.

Even Cooler!

For orange French toast, add 1 teaspoon of orange zest to the egg mixture.

Baked Ham & Eggs

An elegant do-ahead twist
on a favorite combo!

SERVES 8

INGREDIENTS

2 tablespoons butter, plus extra to grease the pan

½ cup finely chopped onion

1 cup chopped broccoli (use only the tops, not the stalks)

1½ cups sliced mushrooms

8 eggs

2 cups whole milk

½ teaspoon salt

⅛ teaspoon ground pepper

Loaf of sliced bread (sourdough or Italian bread works best)

2 cups cooked ham, cut in ½-inch cubes (about 1 pound)

3 cups grated Cheddar cheese

TOOLS:

Cutting board	Mixing bowls	Grater	Waxed paper
Small sharp knife	Spoon	Prep bowls	Plastic wrap
Measuring cups	Whisk	Skillet	Pot holder
Measuring spoons	9 × 13 pan	Spatula	

1. Melt the butter in a skillet over medium-high heat. Add the onion, broccoli, and mushrooms and cook for 5 minutes. Remove the pan from the heat and put the mixture in a prep bowl. Mix in the cubed ham.

2. Whisk the eggs, milk, salt, and pepper together until blended.

3. Grease the bottom and sides of a 9 × 13 pan with butter.

4. Place a layer of bread slices in the pan. Cover the bread with half the vegetable and ham mixture. Sprinkle 1 cup of cheese evenly over the top.

5. Repeat step four. Use all the remaining vegetable and ham mixture and top it with another layer of bread.

6. Pour the egg mixture evenly over everything. Cover the pan with plastic wrap and refrigerate it overnight.

7. In the morning, preheat the oven to 350 degrees. Remove the plastic wrap from the pan and sprinkle the remaining 1 cup of cheese over the top of the bread.

8. Bake for 1 hour, or until the mixture is bubbling and the top is golden brown.

Variations

> Make a vegetarian version by **omitting** the ham and using an additional 2 cups of vegetables.

> For a richer version, add 8 ounces of cubed cream cheese to the vegetable mixture.

> Use chopped red and green peppers instead of broccoli.

> Top the cooked dish with chopped scallions and serve it with sour cream on the side.

Crazy Cranberry Scones

Everyone goes crazy over these classic pastries!

INGREDIENTS

2 cups all-purpose flour
1/3 cup plus 1 tablespoon sugar
1 tablespoon baking powder
1/2 teaspoon salt
6 tablespoons cold butter
2/3 cup dried cranberries
1 teaspoon grated orange zest
1 egg
1/2 cup plus 1 tablespoon heavy cream
1 tablespoon sugar

TOOLS: Measuring cups, Measuring spoons, Prep bowls, Zester, Mixing bowl, Pastry blender, Fork, Waxed paper, Table knife, Baking sheet, Pastry brush, Pot holder, Wire rack

26

1. Preheat the oven to 425 degrees.

2. Whisk the flour, ⅓ cup of sugar, salt, and baking powder together in a mixing bowl.

3. Cut the butter into ½-inch cubes. Add it to the dry ingredients in the mixing bowl.

4. Use a **pastry** blender to cut the butter into the dry ingredients. If you don't have a pastry blender, use two table knives instead. Work the mixture until it forms pea-size pieces. The texture needs to be coarse, so do not make a paste or a smooth mixture!

5. Add the cranberries and orange zest to the bowl and mix them in with a fork.

6. Mix the egg and ½ cup of cream in a prep bowl with a fork. Add the egg mixture to the mixing bowl and stir with a fork until everything is moistened.

7. Use your hands to work the mixture into a ball. Knead the dough about 10 times in the bowl. Move the ball of dough to a sheet of waxed paper.

8. Flatten the dough ball into a circle about 10 inches across. Cut it into 8 wedges using a table knife.

9. Put the wedges on a baking sheet and brush the tops with the remaining 1 tablespoon of cream. Sprinkle the remaining 1 tablespoon of sugar over the tops.

10. Bake the scones for 12 minutes, or until the tops are lightly browned. Cool them on a wire rack.

Great Granola!

MAKES ABOUT 10 CUPS

Nutty nutrition in a delicious breakfast cereal!

INGREDIENTS

5 cups rolled oats
1 cup flaked coconut
1 cup cashew pieces
1 cup sunflower seeds
½ cup wheat germ
½ cup sesame seeds
⅔ cup brown sugar
⅓ cup honey
⅔ cup cooking oil
1½ cups raisins

TOOLS: Measuring cups   Large mixing bowl   Rubber spatula   Pot holder
Prep bowls   Saucepan   Baking sheet

1 Preheat the oven to 325 degrees.

2 Mix the oats, coconut, cashew pieces, sunflower seeds, wheat germ, and sesame seeds in a large mixing bowl.

3 Put the brown sugar and honey in a saucepan. Cook over medium heat, stirring constantly until the sugar dissolves.

4 Pour the sugar mixture and the cooking oil over the dry ingredients. Mix with a rubber spatula until all the dry ingredients are coated.

5 Spread the mixture on a baking sheet. To keep the granola from burning, keep it away from the sides of the baking sheet.

6 Bake for 40 minutes. Every 10 minutes, remove the pan from the oven and stir the mixture so it bakes evenly. Remember to keep the granola away from the sides of the pan. The granola will be golden brown when it is done.

7 Remove the pan from the oven and spread the granola on foil to cool.

8 When the granola is cool, put it in a large mixing bowl and mix in the raisins.

9 Serve the granola topped with milk and, if you like, sliced fresh fruit.

Variations

> Use your favorite dried fruit in place of the raisins. Good choices include dried cranberries, cherries, golden raisins, apples, blueberries, and yogurt-covered raisins.

> For cinnamon-flavored granola, add ½ teaspoon of cinnamon to the brown sugar and honey mixture.

Breakfast Parfaits

A great breakfast in a glass, and pretty too!

INGREDIENTS

FOR YOGURT PARFAIT

1 cup Great Granola!
(page 28)

1½ cups fruit-flavored yogurt

FOR FRUIT PARFAIT

1 cup Great Granola!
(page 28)

1½ cups Rainbow Fruit Salad
(page 18)

1 Put ¼ cup of fruit salad or yogurt in the bottom of each glass. Sprinkle ¼ cup of granola over the top.

2 Repeat the layers, ending with fruit salad or yogurt on top. If you like, sprinkle a small amount of granola on top for a garnish.

TOOLS: Measuring cups
Spoon

Glossary

complement – to complete or bring to perfection.

guava – a sweet, pear-shaped tropical fruit.

omit – to leave out.

pastry – a sweet, baked food.

serrated – having a jagged edge.

yolk – the yellow inner portion of a bird or reptile egg.

Web Sites

To learn more about cool cooking, visit ABDO Publishing Company on the World Wide Web at **www.abdopublishing.com**. Web sites about cool cooking are featured on our Book Links page. These links are routinely monitored and updated to provide the most current information available.

Index